Boo-Boo's New Leg

A True Story of Illness, Acceptance, and Healing

Written and Illustrated by

Mary Garcia

AuthorHouse™
1663 Liberty Drive
Bloomington, IN 47403
www.authorhouse.com
Phone: 1-800-839-8640

©2011 Mary E. Garcia. All rights reserved.

No part of this book may be reproduced, stored in a retrieval system, or transmitted by any means without the written permission of the author.

First published by AuthorHouse 1/17/2011

ISBN: 978-1-4567-1545-8 (sc)

Library of Congress Control Number: 2010919303

Printed in the United States of America

Any people depicted in stock imagery provided by Thinkstock are models, and such images are being used for illustrative purposes only.
Certain stock imagery © Thinkstock.

This book is printed on acid-free paper.

Because of the dynamic nature of the Internet, any Web addresses or links contained in this book may have changed since publication and may no longer be valid. The views expressed in this work are solely those of the author and do not necessarily reflect the views of the publisher, and the publisher hereby disclaims any responsibility for them.

Bear illustrations based on Build-A-Bear Workshop, Inc. bear designs © 1999 Build-A-Bear Workshop, Inc. Reproduced with permission. All rights reserved.

My FORMULA for the successful completion of this book:

1. A LOVING and SUPPORTIVE extended family- and believe me there are so many of them who've given great advice and help, especially my parents Matt and Terry and my mother-in-law, Rosie, who helped us through rough financial times so I could begin and continue working on the book.
2. Having a muse. Jennifer (and her husband Sal) taught me how to accept the bad things in life with a smile and a laugh and that pain is never easy but there is always joy in life to savor.
3. A child named Sara whose adorable nickname for Jennifer continues to this day and inspired the story to be written. Also, Allison who let me depict both herself and her children Sara and Ryan in the story.
4. Jennifer's brother Dave and his son Alex who also let me feature them.
5. My friend Ida who every week threatened to kick my butt if I didn't publish this story I wrote with pencil on loose leaf paper.
6. Finding AuthorHouse publishing who did everything at my pace and creative instruction.
7. My wonderful kids, Robert and Emma who took the job of being my models for the illustrations, even when it embarrassed them.
8. My cousin Karen and Uncle Reuben who gave me work on the weekends to help with the educational needs of my son at exactly the right moment.
9. A "certain social network" of friends, old and new, who always encouraged me.
10. Enduring prayers on my behalf to the ONE above.
11. My cousin Diane whose talent provided me with a great author photograph.
12. My sister Jennifer's honest and loving critique of my work which led me to create the best quality artwork this story deserved.
13. My AWESOME husband Joe who made lots of my work time possible and picked up a lot of slack at home and with the kids. Without his support this would never have been possible.

Thank You

This book is dedicated to the memory of Jennifer's parents, George and Roseann Freed.

Hi, my name is Sara, and this is Boo-Boo. She's my special friend. We do all kinds of things together. We play together, shop together, have sleepovers, and even go on vacations together. She has something that most of us don't. Do you want to know why I call her Boo-Boo? Well, it's because she had the very first boo-boo I can ever remember seeing.

Everyone gets boo-boos. It happens every now and then. You probably fell off of your bike when you were learning to ride and scraped your elbow or knee. My brother Ryan and I have done that. Maybe you were running in your house and tripped and bumped your head. We've done that too. Our mom and dad cleaned lots of scrapes and covered lots of bumps, but some of those times we still felt lousy. This boo-boo that I'm talking about is different. It didn't just happen all of a sudden, and it didn't just ruin my friend's day; it changed her whole life.

One day when I was almost two years old, I was playing blocks with my friend Robbie at Boo-Boo's house. He saw that there were lots of bandages on her foot. He pointed to it and called out, "Boo-boo!" I copied him. "Boo-boo!" I shouted. "Boo-boo! Boo-boo!" we both shouted. Then every time I saw her with the bandages, I would call out, "Boo-boo!" That's the name I gave her. I still call her Boo-Boo now that I'm almost eleven years old. Even when my little brother Ryan was learning to talk, I taught him to call her by this name. Boo-Boo loves it.

As Boo-Boo's pain got worse, her husband, Sal, had to leave his job for good so he could stay home and take care of her. Standing and walking became very hard for her, so he had to buy her a walker and a chair for the shower. I had already stopped using a walker and a bathtub chair, and now Boo-Boo was using her own. Her walker was much bigger than mine was, though.

Sometimes I would hide under the walker and Uncle Sal would throw a blanket over it to make a clubhouse for me. Of course, we only did this when Boo-Boo wasn't using it.

Boo-Boo went on many doctor visits. She also stayed home a lot. She just couldn't get comfy anymore. Sometimes she cried. Back then I thought only babies and kids cried. I found out that grown-ups do too. I love Boo-Boo so much, and it made me sad to see her cry. She had to go stay at the hospital so her doctors could help her get better.

One September day at the hospital, the doctors operated on Boo-Boo's foot. They took off her toes because they were very sick. They just would not get better no matter what else they tried. This kind of operation is called an amputation (amp-you-tay-shun). I know this sounds scary, but since all of the sickness was in her toes, it was better to take away the bad stuff before it made her whole body sick.

Boo-Boo stayed in the hospital for a few weeks. It was the worst time in her life. Even after the operation, her foot hurt very much. My mommy took me there to visit her on one of her good days. There were many strange things in her hospital room. Wires and machines kept beeping, and there were flashing lights. She had a needle in her hand that was connected to a long tube that led to a medicine-filled bag hanging on a metal pole.

Boo-Boo rested there while many nurses and doctors took care of her. She started to feel a little better every day. Uncle Sal couldn't wait to take her home where she would be most comfy.

Boo-Boo had to use a wheelchair and crutches for a while. She couldn't wait to stand and walk on her own. These things helped her get around easier.

When she healed up, she went to a special doctor called a prosthetist (prahs-thi-tist).

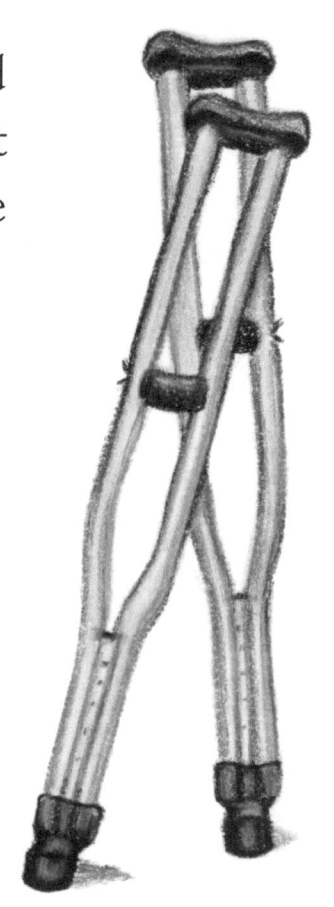

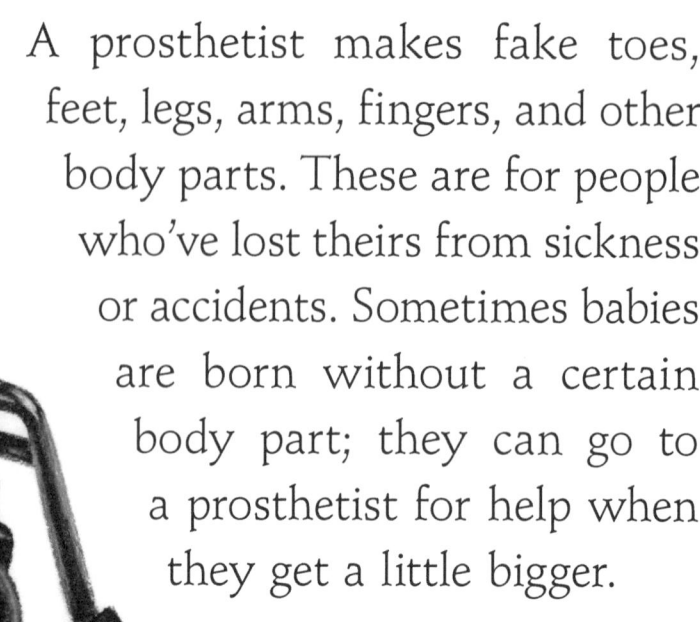

A prosthetist makes fake toes, feet, legs, arms, fingers, and other body parts. These are for people who've lost theirs from sickness or accidents. Sometimes babies are born without a certain body part; they can go to a prosthetist for help when they get a little bigger.

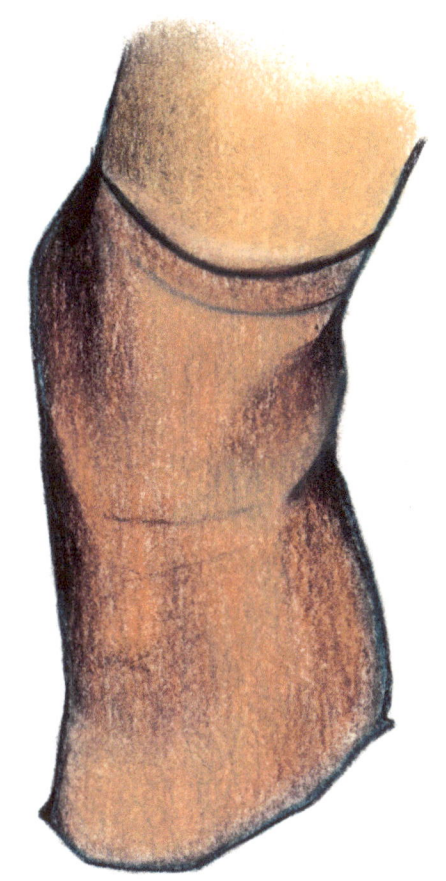

Boo-Boo's prosthetist made her some fake toes to wear on her foot. This is called a toe prosthesis (prahs-thee-sis).

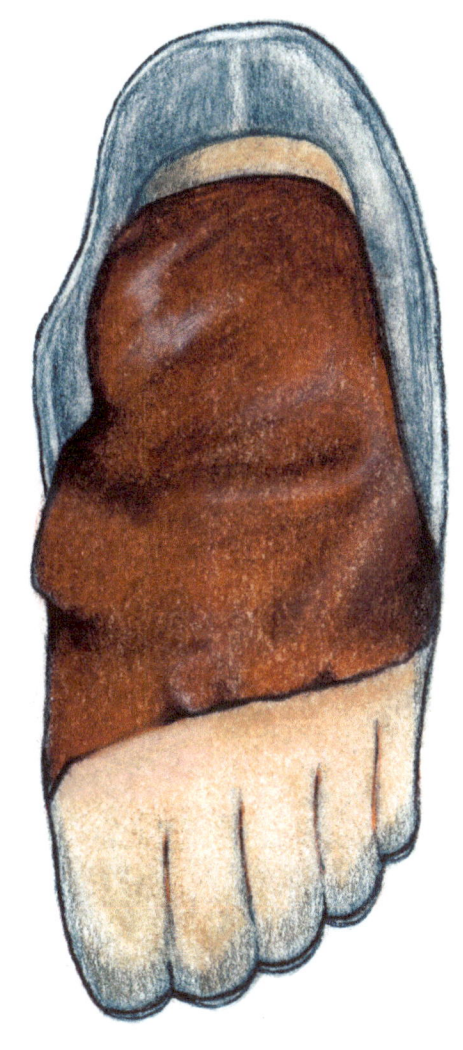

They were made of plastic, leather, and foam, like some of my toys. She didn't like them at first, but the doctor told Boo-Boo she would get used to wearing them, and she did!

For a while it seemed that Boo-Boo was all better, but then her sickness came back. Her foot started to hurt badly again. Uncle Sal had to take her back to the doctor. They gave her medicine to help her pain, but it didn't always work.

I tried to make her smile with songs and drawings. I even danced and told her jokes.

But sometimes Boo-Boo just couldn't smile.

Boo-Boo had to go back to the hospital for a while.

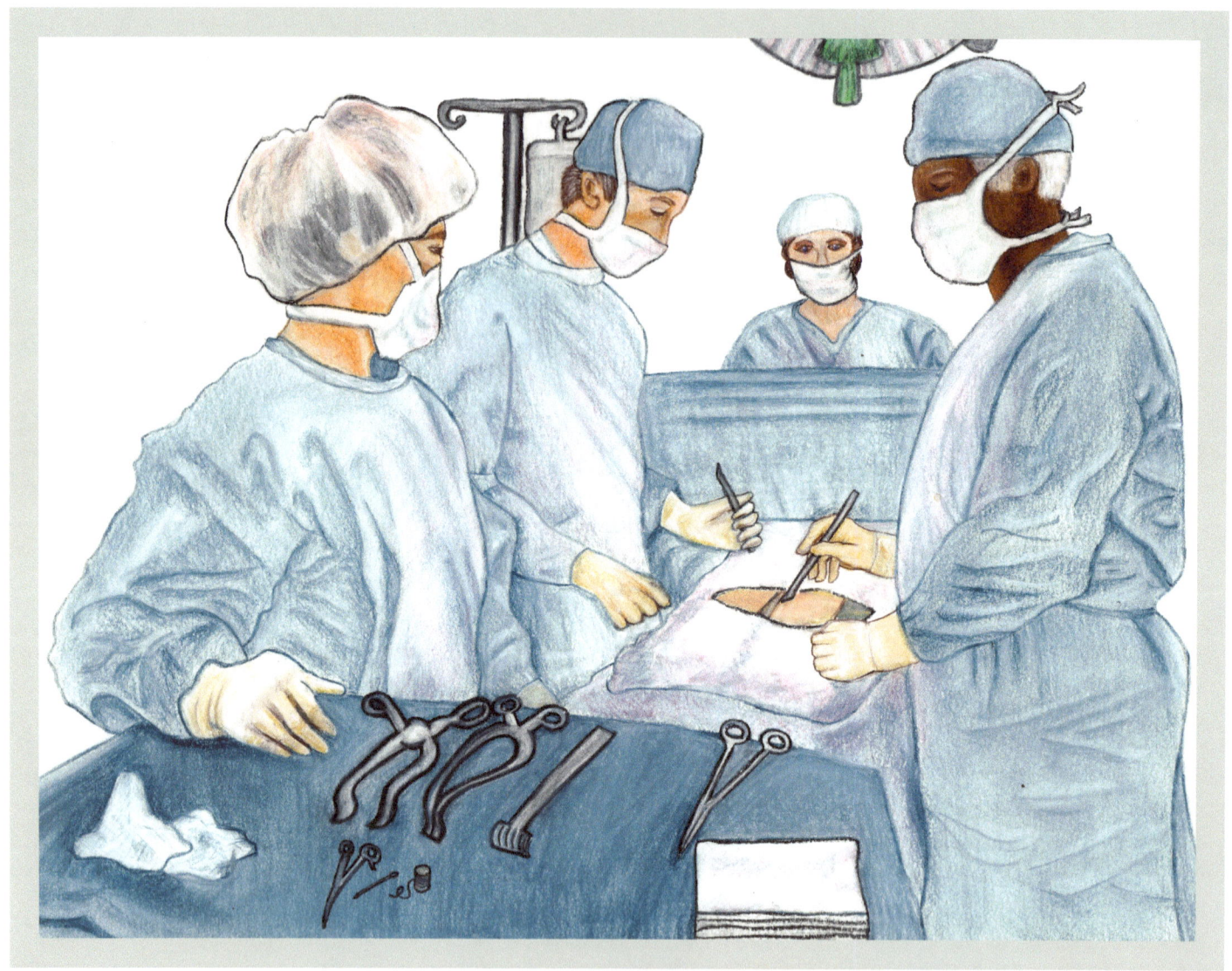

On Halloween Day, the doctors did another operation. This time they took off her whole foot and part of her leg, too. It was another amputation (amp-you-tay-shun). I know this sounds even scarier than before, but keeping her foot would have made her whole body too sick to live. Even Boo-Boo agreed with the doctors that it should be done. Actually, she couldn't wait for them to do it, even as scared as she was. This time she didn't feel as bad after the operation. She was happy that the sickness was gone for good!

After Boo-Boo's leg healed from the operation, I went to visit her at home. She was covered by a blanket on the couch. For a while I just sat on the couch with her and looked at the flat space under the blanket. "Can I see it?" I asked her. She pulled back the blanket, and I saw it for the first time. "Not bad," I said. She nodded her head and said, "Yeah, not bad at all."

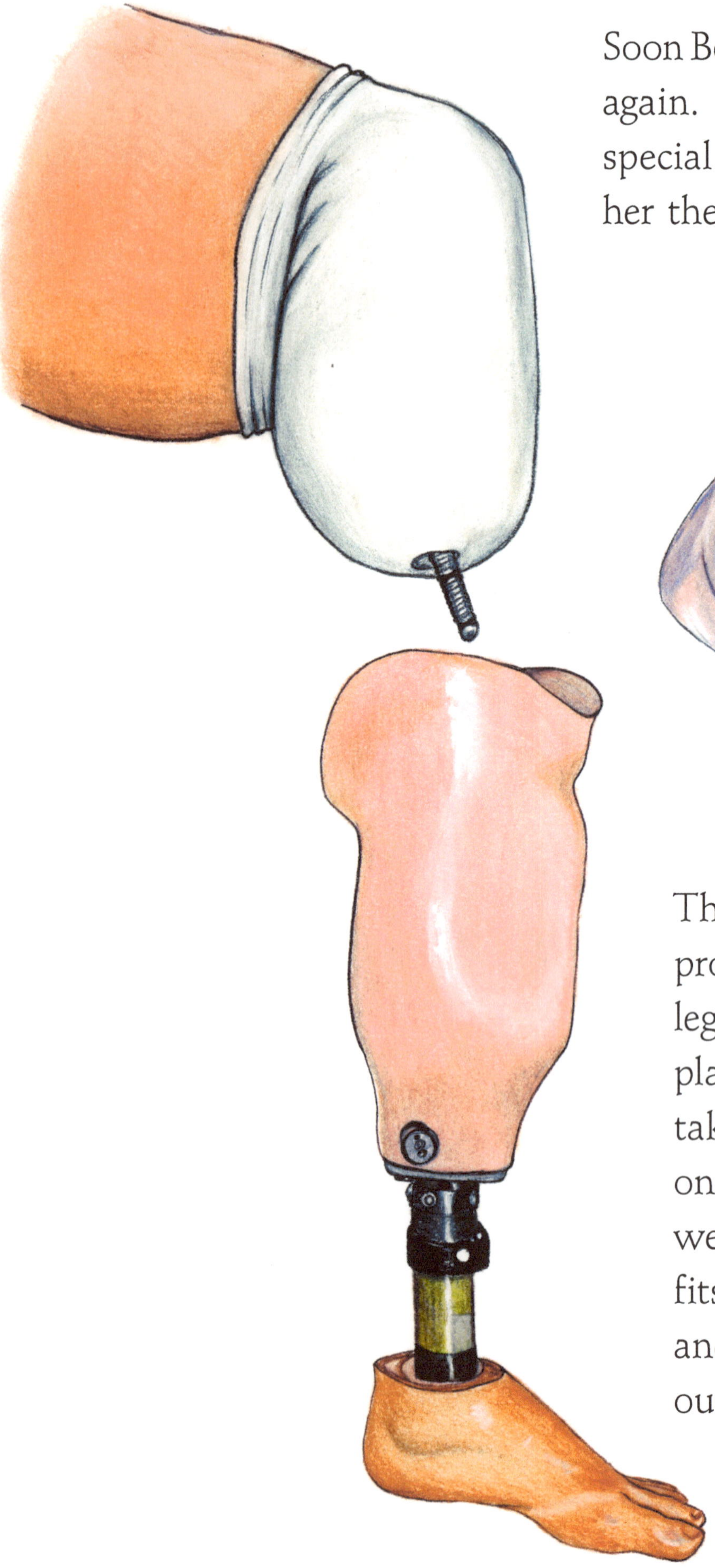

Soon Boo-Boo felt very healthy again. She went back to the special doctor who had given her the fake toes.

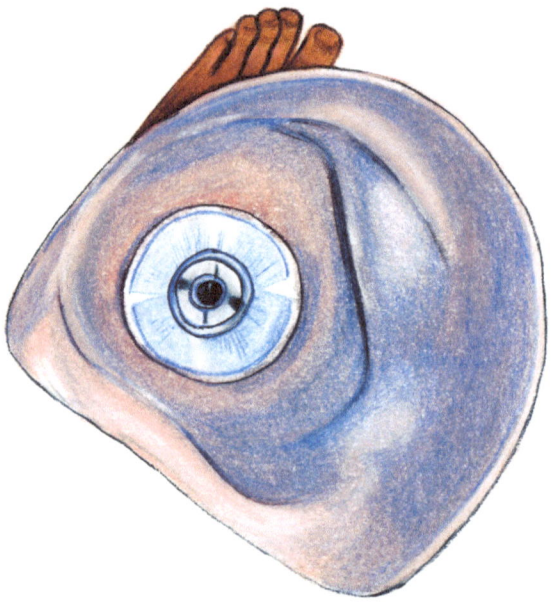

This time he gave her a leg prosthesis. This is a special leg that is made of metal, plastic, and rubber. She can take it off and put it back on very easily. She has to wear a knee sleeve, which fits like a tight rubber glove and has a pin sticking right out of the middle.

It makes a click-click-click sound when it locks into place. Sometimes I step on her fake foot and she yells, "Ouch!" and we both giggle.

Boo-Boo eventually grew out of that first leg and had to be fitted for a new one. It fits the same way the first one did. There's no metal pole above the ankle, so it looks a lot more like a real leg. She has to wear a special stocking over it to keep it clean and protected. Sometimes I see her wearing a long skirt and forget that she has a fake leg.

One day Boo-Boo will have to be fitted for a third leg. She told me that our bodies are always changing, so we need to shop for new clothes and even new prosthetics (prahs-thet-iks) from time to time.

On the first anniversary of her amputation, Boo-Boo went to a costume party dressed as a pirate! Everyone thought it was very funny that she chose that costume, because lots of pirates in stories had fake legs too. She made everyone smile. I imagined Captain Boo-Boo with her parrot on her shoulder and a treasure chest waiting to be opened.

Boo-Boo never gets upset about having a fake leg. She sometimes jokes about it with her close friends. She's gotten some really funny presents from Uncle Sal since then, and she loved them more than anything. He had a special amputee (amp-you-tee) teddy bear made for her at my favorite stuffed animal store. It's so cute. It wears a velvet jogging suit, and one leg is much shorter than the other, just like Boo-Boo's. We call the bear Baby Boo-Boo. I play with it every time I visit. And, since she loves chocolate so much, Uncle Sal gave her a little milk chocolate leg too. Boo-Boo laughed hard just before she gobbled it up!

Since she had not gone back to work yet, Boo-Boo helped my mommy and our friend Mary by being their nanny. I was so happy to see Boo-Boo more often. While she watched us, my brother Ryan and I would try on the fake leg or carry it around. Robbie would pretend to have a third leg with it and baby Emma would stir toys in it with a spoon. We all had fun with Boo-Boo's new leg.

The coolest thing happened the day we went to the arcade with Boo-Boo's nephew, Alex. He was sitting at a driving game and couldn't reach the gas pedal. Boo-Boo took off her leg and said, "Here, this should help." I couldn't wait for my turn!

One thing Boo-Boo really misses is swimming in the ocean. She told me she used to go to the beach with my mommy and me all the time before her amputations. Now she can't get her leg prosthesis (prahs-thee-sis) wet. She needs a special leg for that. When she finally gets one, she'll be our "Aqua Boo-Boo!" We won't be scared to go in the ocean with Aqua Boo-Boo by our sides!

Besides the water legs, there are also special legs for women who want to wear high-heeled shoes. Boo-Boo hasn't worn this kind of shoe in a very long time.

Both of the special legs cost a lot of money. Boo-Boo has to save her money for a long time so she can buy them. I couldn't fit that much money into my piggy bank.

She is going to take me shoe shopping with her, and we'll have such a great time. I can hardly wait. After all these years, Boo-Boo will be so excited to see those fancy shoes on her feet. She'll probably want to go out dancing afterward.

These days, Boo-Boo works in an office. She types on a computer and talks to lots of people from all over the world. She's a great saleslady. I am so happy for her. She is smart and strong, sweet and funny. I'm glad she's all better. She never gave up believing she would get well. She's got everything she needs in life to make her feel safe and happy. Every Halloween we now celebrate the day that Boo-Boo's boo-boo finally got better!

About the Author

Author photograph by Diane Kapllani, 2010

Mary Garcia has always had a fascination for children's books. She can often times be found in the children's section of her local library admiring the artwork in them, getting lost in the stories. She attended Suffolk County Community College where she developed a love of painting, illustrating, calligraphy and photography. Told by her friends that she possesses a Martha- Stewart-esque type of creativity, Mary creates on a daily basis. She became interested in writing children's books from sharing and observing the experiences of those around her. She says she "owe's her unending gratitude to her family and friends for much needed emotional support and motivation through many of her projects". She lives in Long Island, NY with her husband and two children who never cease to make her laugh and inspire new ideas.

Lightning Source UK Ltd.
Milton Keynes UK
UKHW021733090622
404153UK00002B/72